HABITATS OF THE WORLD

DESERTS

ALISON BALLANCE

DOMINIE PRESS
Pearson Learning Group

About Deserts

A desert is a very dry place. There are many different kinds of deserts.

Deserts can be hot or cold, sandy or stony.

Deserts are dry because very little rain falls on them. Dry winds quickly suck water away. Deserts get very hot during the day. You have to be tough to live in a desert.

The Sahara Desert

The Sahara Desert, which is in Africa, is a sandy desert. It is the biggest desert in the world. It is also the hottest. The Sahara has very big sand dunes.

The Gobi Desert

The Gobi Desert is the largest desert in Asia. The Gobi is farther away from the sea than any other place on earth. Winters are very cold in the Gobi Desert, and the ground there is stony.

The Atacama Desert

The Atacama Desert, in Chile, is the driest place in the world. In some parts of this desert, it hasn't rained in more than 400 years.

Camels

Camels are the biggest animals in the desert. They can **survive** for ten days without drinking. Camels have humps on their backs. They store fat in the humps. They have long eyelashes to keep sand out of their eyes.

Scorpions

Scorpions are fierce hunters. They hide under rocks during the day and hunt insects at night. Scorpions get all the water they need from the insects they eat.

Gerbils

Gerbils dig lots of **burrows**. Their long burrows are damp and cool under the ground. Gerbils live in big family groups. They get all their water from the plants they eat.

How Desert Plants Survive

It is hard for desert plants to find water. Some desert plants have very long roots that reach down into damp sand. This plant is a **parasite**. That means it steals water and food from the roots of other plants.

Cactuses

Cactuses are **common** in American deserts. They have spines instead of leaves. This helps them to **conserve** water. Some cactuses can grow up to twenty feet tall.

Nomads

Some people who live in deserts are **nomads**. They stay cool by wearing loose clothes. Nomads move around a lot as they look for food and water. They can find water at an oasis, or **permanent** water hole.

Deserts are among the most beautiful — and most barren — habitats on earth.

GLOSSARY

burrow: A hole in the ground dug by an animal and used for shelter

common: Found in many places

conserve: To keep or save for future use

nomads: People who roam from place to place

parasite: A plant or animal that lives by feeding off other plants or animals

permanent: Lasting for a long time

survive: To stay alive

INDEX